COOKING THE
THE
ENGLISH
WAY

Lerner Publications Company,
A division of Lerner Publishing Group
241 First Avenue North
Minneapolis, MN 55401 U.S.A.

Website address: www.lernerbooks.com

Library of Congress Cataloging-in-Publication Data

Hill, Barbara W., 1941–
     Cooking the English way / by Barbara W. Hill.— Rev. & expanded.
        p.   cm. — (Easy menu ethnic cookbooks)
     Includes index.
     ISBN: 0–8225–4105–X (lib. bdg. : alk. paper)
     1. Cookery, English—Juvenile literature. 2. England—Social life and
customs—Juvenile literature. I. Title. II. Series.
     TX717 .H546 2003
     641.5942—dc21   2001006145

Manufactured in the United States of America
1 2 3 4 5 6 – JR – 08 07 06 05 04 03

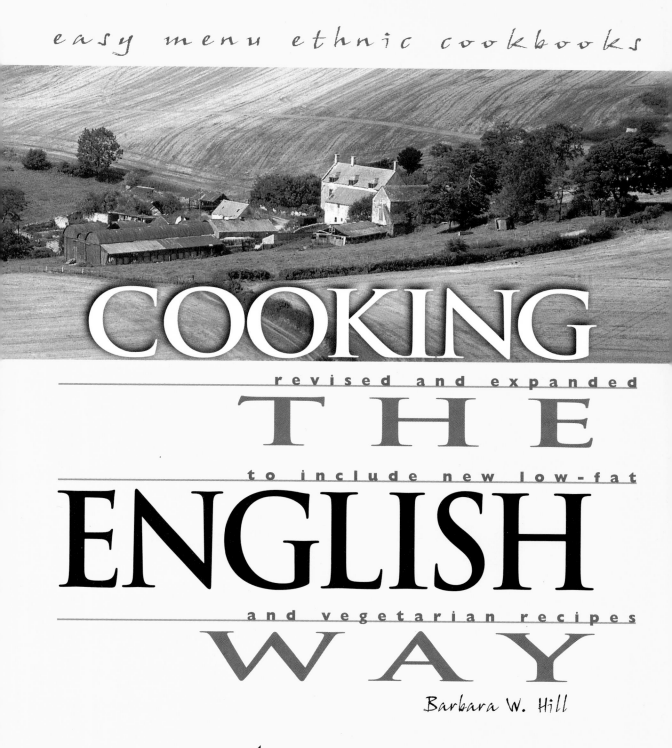

easy menu ethnic cookbooks

COOKING

THE

revised and expanded

ENGLISH

to include new low-fat

and vegetarian recipes

WAY

Barbara W. Hill

Lerner Publications Company • Minneapolis

Contents

Introduction

Fresh-caught fish, tender roast beef, rich scones and shortbread—these are just a few of the varied foods that make up the cooking of England. For years English cuisine was regarded as bland and unexciting. This reputation has changed as English chefs have become more adventurous, earning praise for their innovative and flavorful dishes. Although most English food is not spicy or unusual, it is hearty and delicious. It relies on fresh, simple ingredients prepared to highlight the natural flavors of foods. English cooking also incorporates influences from the many cultures that make up the English population, such as East Asian, West Indian, and Chinese communities.

England is famous for its large cooked breakfast and for afternoon tea, dainty sandwiches and sweets served with a pot of tea. "Takeaway" (takeout) food also got its start in England with fish and chips—pieces of fried cod or haddock and thick French fries served with salt and vinegar. Another early "fast food" was the Cornish

Fall and winter in England can be a cold and rainy time, so hearty autumn hot pot—a vegetarian stew, topped with cheese-flavored scones—can really hit the spot. (Recipe on pages 66–67.)

pasty, meat and vegetables baked in a pastry crust. Pasties started as a way for miners and farmers to carry their lunch to work.

While fast foods and frozen foods remain popular, many English people are becoming more health conscious. Cooks use less fat in preparing food, and people are eating less meat, eggs, butter, and sugar and more fruits, vegetables, and whole-grain bread. The recipes in this book will give you a taste of English cooking that's both good for your health and good tasting.

The Land

England, Wales, and Scotland make up Great Britain (often called simply Britain), and these countries plus Northern Ireland form the United Kingdom. Britain is one of the British Isles, which lie in the North Atlantic Ocean off the northwestern coast of mainland Europe. The English coast stretches for hundreds of miles. It is lined with high cliffs, jagged rocks, and beaches.

England has a damp climate and moderate temperatures. Though it is never very hot or cold, it is often swept by chilly winds and sudden showers. In much of England, frequent rains turn the countryside a brilliant green. Beautiful fields are crisscrossed by hedges and low stone walls. Sheep and cattle graze on lush grasses in the hills and valleys.

Farmland covers much of England. English farmers grow barley, potatoes, wheat, sugar beets, and other crops. Oats are grown in the high, rugged hills and wild moors of northern England. The county of Kent, in the southeast, is called the Garden of England and is famous for its apple and cherry orchards.

The White Cliffs of Dover in Kent draw tourists, as well as locals, to the spectacular chalky landscape overlooking the English Channel.

The Food

Every part of England has its own specialties, from the Cornish pasties of Cornwall to the Lancashire hot pot to Yorkshire pudding. Among the hundreds of regional specialties are gingerbread from the Lake District in northern England; Staffordshire oatcakes, a type of pancake; Cumberland sausage; and apple cider from the West Country (the counties of Somerset, Dorset, Devon, and Cornwall).

Beyond the regional favorites, many foods are commonly eaten throughout England. Sheep have always been important both for their wool and their meat. Lamb is the main ingredient in the Lancashire hot pot, for example, a robust stew from Lancashire, an area of rich, fertile plains in the northwestern part of the country.

Sheep graze on the nutritious grasses of the Lake District.

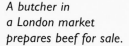

A butcher in a London market prepares beef for sale.

(The meat of a sheep is called lamb if the animal is under eight months old, mutton if it is older.) In addition, spicy dishes from India and the Caribbean, referred to simply as curries, are popular throughout England.

Despite health concerns about British beef in recent years, it is safe to eat and remains a staple of the English diet. Cattle breeds such as the white-faced Hereford are famous for their fine meat. In many English homes, the traditional Sunday meal is a joint, or roast, of beef. It is often served with Yorkshire pudding (a batter baked with the meat drippings), roasted potatoes, and seasonal vegetables. The trimmings—brown gravy and horseradish sauce—are important, too.

People in England eat fish as much as meat. Since no point in the British Isles is more than seventy miles from the sea, fresh fish is available everywhere, all year long. Common types include mackerel, cod, haddock, salmon, and Dover sole. Shellfish, such as crabs, mussels, and oysters, is available in many coastal towns. In the East End of London, street vendors sell dishes of prawns, whelks, and cockles, all sprinkled with malt vinegar.

England also produces outstanding dairy products, including a wealth of local cheeses. The most famous are Cheddar, from the village of Cheddar in the west of England, and Stilton, from a district of the same name in central England. The largest Cheddar cheese ever made weighed 1,100 pounds and was given to Queen Victoria as a wedding present in 1840.

Specialty farmhouse cheeses—such as Stilton, Cotswold, and Cheddar—are favorite fare in England as well as in the United States.

The prize of dairy products is double cream. It is far thicker than American whipping cream—so thick that it has to be spooned, not poured, onto such mouth-watering desserts as summer pudding and trifle, a jam-covered dessert. When double cream is gently heated, it becomes even thicker and is known as clotted cream. In southwestern England, well known for its cream teas, bowls of clotted cream are served with jam and scones. English people have an ongoing debate about whether it's best to put the cream or the jam on the scone first. Either way, it tastes wonderful.

Many English people refer to all desserts as "puddings." In England, a pudding may be many things besides a creamy milk-based dessert. It might be a pie or a sponge cake. It can be hot or cold, but most often it will be hot, to help keep warm in the cold, damp English weather.

Many English recipes have unusual and colorful names. Some examples are bubble and squeak, courting cake, lardy cake, singing hinnies, Sally Lunns, orange fool, Bath chaps, hasty pudding, toad-in-the-hole, mushy peas, salmagundi, angels on horseback, and devils on horseback. As you're having fun experimenting with English cooking, maybe you can invent clever names of your own for your creations.

Holidays and Festivals

Public holidays in Britain are called bank holidays. They include New Year's Day, Good Friday, Easter, the first and last Mondays in May, Christmas, and Boxing Day (December 26). Between Christmas and New Year's, many offices and schools close.

Besides the official bank holidays, people in England celebrate many different occasions throughout the year. Many holidays are connected to the seasons and cycles of the year, such as harvesttime or spring. Other festivals celebrate quirky local traditions, including the Furry Dance, a stately, rhythmic procession of fancily dressed

Participants in the Furry Dance in Cornwall celebrate the coming of spring.

men and women. It takes place on Floral Day (May 8) in the village of Helston in Cornwall.

Christmas is a major holiday in England. In London, a Christmas tree is raised in Trafalgar Square and there's a Christmas parade. Throughout the country, people gather to sing carols during the holiday season. On Christmas Day, many English families pull "crackers" before dinner. These are small tubes covered with bright paper and twisted at the ends. When you pull on the end, the cracker explodes and jokes and paper hats fall out. Family members wear the hats during dinner. Christmas dinner is usually roast turkey, followed by plum pudding.

The day after Christmas is Boxing Day, which was traditionally a time to give money and other gifts to charity, needy families, and people in service jobs. The holiday evolved into a day to spend with family or to get out and play sports.

In the West Country of England, wassailing ceremonies are held around Epiphany, or Twelfth Night—the twelfth night after Christmas, when, according to Christian belief, three kings arrived with gifts for the baby Jesus. The word *wassail* comes from two old Saxon words meaning "good health." The custom is to drink apple cider punch and toast the apple trees to ensure a good crop that year. The West Country has an ideal climate and soil for apple orchards, and the area is famous for its hard, or dry, apple cider, an alcoholic beverage.

Another tradition on Epiphany is to bake a three kings almond tart. A dried bean, gold ring, or tiny baby figurine is hidden in the cake, and a gold cardboard crown is placed on top of the cake. When the tart is served, the person who finds the hidden object is crowned king or queen of the feast for the evening.

Many holidays and festivals in England mark the coming of spring. Easter dates back to ancient times and was later linked to Christianity. The holiday is named after the Anglo-Saxon goddess of the dawn and spring, Eostre or Eastre. Many Easter traditions and symbols have to do with birth, good luck, and fertility.

Lent, the forty-day period before Easter, involves many food traditions. Shrove Tuesday, the day before the start of Lent, is known as Pancake Day in England. People traditionally made pancakes on that day to use up any foods that were forbidden during Lent, such as lard (pork fat). The day was also a time for games and merriment. The celebration was announced in many villages by the ringing of the pancake bell. In some towns, a pancake race still takes place on Shrove Tuesday. Women race with pancakes in frying pans, tossing them as they run.

Easter eggs and chocolate bunnies are part of Easter in England, just as in the United States. In northern England, another custom is egg rolling, in which hard-boiled eggs are rolled down slopes to see whose egg goes farthest. The village of Hallaton in Leicester holds a "hare pie scramble" and bottle kicking contest on Easter Monday. Half of a hare pie (actually a beef pie) is distributed to villagers, and the rest is scrambled, or tossed out to the children. Then the villagers begin a game that involves kicking beer barrels.

In villages near the Severn River in west central England, an elver-eating contest is held on Easter Monday. Elvers are baby eels, which make their way up the river each spring. One champion ate about seven hundred elvers in half a minute!

Another spring festival is May Day, when dancers called morris men, dressed in white clothing decorated with colorful sashes, ribbons, and bells and carrying white handkerchiefs and sticks, perform in village streets. Some villages in Gloucestershire celebrate the spring bank holiday with a cheese rolling. A large round of cheese is packed in a strong wooden case and rolled down a steep hill. Competitors chase after it, and the winner gets to keep the cheese.

The summer and fall bring more festivals. In London, a large street fair called the Notting Hill Carnival takes place during the last weekend in August. It's a spectacular celebration of Afro-Caribbean culture, with floats, music, and hundreds of stalls selling arts and crafts and all sorts of food and drink. In the autumn, harvest festivals take place all over England, especially in farming areas. In Colchester, on the east coast, the Oyster Festival in September celebrates the start of the oyster-fishing season. On September 29, the old holiday of Michaelmas, or the feast of Saint Michael, was traditionally celebrated with a meal of a well-fattened goose that had fed on the stubble of the fields after the harvest. The Nottingham Goose Fair has taken place around this time of the year for more than seven hundred years. Originally, geese were sold at the fair, then walked to London in time to fatten up for Christmas. Although the fair no longer has anything to do with geese, there's plenty of good fair food, along with rides and games.

Many people in England celebrate Halloween, but a more important holiday comes a few days later, on November 5. Guy Fawkes Night, or Bonfire Night, marks the day in 1605 when a man named

Guy Fawkes tried to blow up the Houses of Parliament. Fawkes wanted to kill King James I because he felt the king and his government were treating Roman Catholics unfairly. Fawkes's plot failed, however, and he was hanged.

Throughout England on Guy Fawkes Night, fireworks are set off and people light bonfires. They make dummies called guys out of straw and old clothes. The guy is tossed into the fire and burned. Gingerbread is traditionally eaten around the bonfire on Guy Fawkes Night.

Whether it's for a holiday, special occasion, or just an everyday meal, you can cook up some tasty English treats to impress your family and friends. Cheers!

Guy Fawkes Night is an occasion for fireworks and bonfires.

Before You Begin

Cooking any dish, plain or fancy, is easier and more fun if you are familiar with its ingredients. English cooking makes use of some ingredients that you may not know. Sometimes special cookware is also used, although the recipes in this book can easily be prepared with ordinary utensils and pans.

The most important thing you need to know before you start is how to be a careful cook. On the following page, you'll find a few rules that will make your cooking experience safe, fun, and easy. Next, take a look at the "dictionary" of cooking utensils, terms, and special ingredients. You may also want to read the section on preparing healthy, low-fat meals.

Once you've picked out a recipe to try, read through it from beginning to end. Now you are ready to shop for ingredients and to organize the cookware you will need. When you have assembled everything, you're ready to begin cooking.

Gingerbread is popular throughout northern England, where it was originally made with oats instead of flour. (Recipe on page 68.)

The Careful Cook

Whenever you cook, there are certain safety rules you must always keep in mind. Even experienced cooks follow these rules when they are in the kitchen.

- Always wash your hands before handling food. Thoroughly wash all raw vegetables and fruits to remove dirt, chemicals, and insecticides. Wash uncooked poultry, fish, and meat under cold water.
- Use a cutting board when cutting up vegetables and fruits. Don't cut them up in your hand! And be sure to cut in a direction *away* from you and your fingers.
- Long hair or loose clothing can easily catch fire if brought near the burners of a stove. If you have long hair, tie it back before you start cooking.
- Turn all pot handles toward the back of the stove so that you will not catch your sleeves or jewelry on them. This is especially important when younger brothers and sisters are around. They could easily knock off a pot and get burned.
- Always use a pot holder to steady hot pots or to take pans out of the oven. Don't use a wet cloth on a hot pan because the steam it produces could burn you.
- Lift the lid of a steaming pot with the opening away from you so that you will not get burned.
- If you get burned, hold the burn under cold running water. Do not put grease or butter on it. Cold water helps to take the heat out, but grease or butter will only keep it in.
- If grease or cooking oil catches fire, throw baking soda or salt at the bottom of the flame to put it out. (Water will *not* put out a grease fire.) Call for help, and try to turn all the stove burners to "off."

Cooking Utensils

baster—A long hollow utensil with a rubber bulb at the end, used to draw liquid out of a pan and for basting

electric mixer—An appliance, either freestanding or handheld, used for mixing and beating

meat thermometer—A thermometer that is inserted into meat or poultry to check how well-done the meat is. Some meat thermometers are left in the whole time the meat cooks, while others are used at intervals.

Cooking Terms

baste—To pour or spoon liquid over food as it roasts in order to flavor and moisten it

broil—To cook directly under a heat source so that the side of the food facing the heat cooks rapidly

cream—To blend dry and wet ingredients until frothy

cut in—A way to combine a solid fat, such as butter, and flour using your fingers, a pastry blender, or two knives. Cut or break the fat into small pieces and mix them with the flour until mixture has a coarse, mealy consistency.

knead—To work dough by pressing it with the palms, pushing it outward, and then pressing it over on itself

pinch—A very small amount, usually what you can pick up between your thumb and forefinger

roast—To cook in an open pan in an oven so that heat penetrates the food from all sides

sauté—To fry quickly over high heat in oil or fat, stirring or turning the food to prevent burning

separate—To divide one ingredient into two or more parts that will be used separately, such as egg yolk and egg white

simmer—To cook over low heat in liquid kept just below its boiling point. Bubbles may occasionally rise to the surface.

whip—To beat ingredients at high speed until mixture is light and fluffy

Special Ingredients

allspice—The dried berry of the West Indian allspice tree, used whole or ground to give a pungent flavor to foods

cloves—The highly fragrant dried flower buds of a tropical tree, used whole or ground as a spice

coriander—The dried seeds of the coriander plant, used whole or ground to give a sweet, spicy flavor to foods

cornstarch—A fine white starch made from corn, commonly used to thicken sauces and gravies

currants—Small, dried, seedless grapes similar to raisins

dry mustard—A powder, made from the ground seeds of the mustard plant, that is used to flavor food

ginger—A plant root that can be used dried or ground in many kinds of recipes, including stir-fries and baked goods

nutmeg—A fragrant spice, either whole or ground, that is often used in desserts

oregano—The dried leaves, whole or powdered, of a rich and fragrant herb that is used as a seasoning in cooking

parsnip—A vegetable that looks something like a white carrot, with a sweet, pungent taste

rosemary—The strongly flavored dried leaves of an herb in the mint family, used as a seasoning for meat, fish, and other dishes

superfine sugar—Sugar that is similar to common granulated white sugar but with finer grains

thyme—The leaves of a bushy shrub that grows mainly in California and France. It is used as an herb in cooking and has a very strong flavor.

tofu—Fresh soybean curd, sold in cakes. Plain tofu tastes bland, but it absorbs flavor from other foods readily. It is a good source of protein.

vegetable shortening—White, solid vegetable fat. It is often used to make pie crust.

vegetable stock—A broth made by simmering vegetables in water until they are soft and their flavors and nutrients have been released into the liquid. Vegetable stock may be homemade or purchased canned or in concentrated form.

whole wheat flour—Flour made without removing bran from the grain

Healthy and Low-Fat Cooking Tips

Many cooks are concerned about preparing healthy, low-fat meals. Fortunately, there are simple ways to reduce the fat content of most dishes. Here are a few general tips for adapting the recipes in this book. Throughout the book, you'll also find specific suggestions for individual recipes—and don't worry, they'll still taste delicious!

Many English recipes call for butter, cream, and other high-fat dairy products. Using oil in place of butter for frying or sautéeing lowers saturated fat in itself, but you can also reduce the amount of oil you use. Sprinkling a little salt on fish or vegetables brings out their natural juices, so less oil is needed. It's also a good idea to use a small, nonstick frying pan if you decide to use less oil than the recipe calls for.

Another common substitute for butter is margarine. Before making this substitution, consider the recipe. If it is a dessert, it's often best to use butter rather than margarine or oil, which may noticeably change the taste or consistency of the food. An easy way to trim fat from a recipe is to use skim milk in place of cream or whole milk.

Many English recipes call for beef or mutton. To reduce fat, buy extra-lean meat. English cooking also uses a lot of fish, which is naturally low in fat.

There are many ways to prepare meals that are good for you and still taste great. As you become a more experienced cook, try experimenting with recipes and substitutions to find the methods that work best for you.

METRIC CONVERSIONS

Cooks in the United States measure both liquid and solid ingredients using standard containers based on the 8-ounce cup and the tablespoon. These measurements are based on volume, while the metric system of measurement is based on both weight (for solids) and volume (for liquids). To convert from U.S. fluid tablespoons, ounces, quarts, and so forth to metric liters is a straightforward conversion, using the chart below. However, since solids have different weights—one cup of rice does not weigh the same as one cup of grated cheese, for example—many cooks who use the metric system have kitchen scales to weigh different ingredients. The chart below will give you a good starting point for basic conversions to the metric system.

MASS (weight)

1 ounce (oz.)	=	28.0 grams (g)
8 ounces	=	227.0 grams
1 pound (lb.) or 16 ounces	=	0.45 kilograms (kg)
2.2 pounds	=	1.0 kilogram

LIQUID VOLUME

1 teaspoon (tsp.)	=	5.0 milliliters (ml)
1 tablespoon (tbsp.)	=	15.0 milliliters
1 fluid ounce (oz.)	=	30.0 milliliters
1 cup (c.)	=	240 milliliters
1 pint (pt.)	=	480 milliliters
1 quart (qt.)	=	0.95 liters (l)
1 gallon (gal.)	=	3.80 liters

LENGTH

¼ inch (in.)	=	0.6 centimeters (cm)
½ inch	=	1.25 centimeters
1 inch	=	2.5 centimeters

TEMPERATURE

212°F	=	100°C (boiling point of water)
225°F	=	110°C
250°F	=	120°C
275°F	=	135°C
300°F	=	150°C
325°F	=	160°C
350°F	=	180°C
375°F	=	190°C
400°F	=	200°C

(To convert temperature in Fahrenheit to Celsius, subtract 32 and multiply by .56)

PAN SIZES

8-inch cake pan	=	20 x 4-centimeter cake pan
9-inch cake pan	=	23 x 3.5-centimeter cake pan
11 x 7-inch baking pan	=	28 x 18-centimeter baking pan
13 x 9-inch baking pan	=	32.5 x 23-centimeter baking pan
9 x 5-inch loaf pan	=	23 x 13-centimeter loaf pan
2-quart casserole	=	2-liter casserole

An English Table

In England many people eat a quick breakfast of cereal and toast and grab lunch at a pub. Pubs are the central meeting spots in many neighborhoods and towns. Pubs serve simple, satisfying meals along with pints of beer and other beverages. But for Sunday lunch, holidays, birthdays, and other special occasions, English families are likely to slow down for a leisurely, more elegant meal.

Teatime is an important English custom. At about 4:00 each afternoon, many people pause for a soothing cup of hot tea and a bite to eat. Afternoon tea can range from a simple cup of tea to a formal meal that includes sandwiches, scones, and a variety of cakes and tarts. At a formal tea, the cakes and sandwiches are served on fine china, and the table may be decorated with a pretty tablecloth, silver utensils, and fresh flowers. At some fancy hotels, the serving of the tea is even accompanied by an orchestra.

Friends gather at a tea shop to enjoy traditional English tea and cakes.

An English Menu

Many people in England shop for food every day rather than once a week, to get the freshest ingredients possible. Although there are plenty of large supermarkets, many English cooks choose to go to a butcher for meat and poultry, to a fish stall or market for fresh fish, to a bakery for bread and pastries, and to an outdoor market for fresh fruits and vegetables. Below are menu plans for tea and supper, along with shopping lists of items that you'll need to prepare these meals.

TEA

Tea

Shortbread

Scones

Victoria sandwich with chocolate frosting

SHOPPING LIST:

Dairy/Egg/Meat

1 stick unsalted butter
eggs
milk or buttermilk
margerine
butter

Canned/Bottled/Boxed

tea*
currants or raisins

Miscellaneous

sugar
superfine sugar
flour
baking powder
salt
cocoa
powdered sugar

*For an authentic English pot of tea, look for an English brand of tea in your supermarket. Check the label or tin to see where the tea comes from. If possible, get loose tea rather than tea bags.

SUNDAY LUNCH

Roast beef

Browned roast potatoes

Yorkshire pudding

Summer pudding

SHOPPING LIST:

Produce

8 medium-sized potatoes

Dairy/Egg/Meat

3½- to 4-lb. boneless sirloin roast, rolled and tied
vegetable shortening
1 egg
milk
whipped cream or nondairy topping

Canned/Bottled/Boxed

10 oz. frozen unsweetened raspberries
10 oz. frozen unsweetened strawberries
1 lb. frozen unsweetened blackberries

Miscellaneous

salt
pepper
flour
baking powder
sugar
1 loaf of white bread

Breakfast

A traditional British breakfast is known for its amazing size and variety. It can include hot or cold cereal, fruit, juice, a "fry-up" of bacon, sausage, mushrooms, tomatoes, and bread—and, of course, eggs. To complete the meal, add a pot of steaming tea or coffee and hot buttered toast with marmalade. In the past, this filling meal gave laborers and farmers fuel for a long day of hard work. These days, most families eat a smaller breakfast, such as cereal and toast, pancakes or oatcakes (a pancake that looks like a scone or biscuit), or yogurt and fruit. But every once in a while, it's a treat to have a big breakfast.

In some English households, breakfast can be a major meal that includes eggs, meat, and cereal. Simpler breakfast fare might be a serving of mushrooms on toast. (Recipe on page 33.)

Fried Bread

This is a favorite accompaniment to eggs and bacon. After you have fried the bacon, keep the fat in the pan hot.

⅓ c. milk

4 slices white or wheat bread

fat for cooking*

1. Brush a little milk on both sides of each piece of bread.
2. In a medium-sized frying pan, melt enough fat to cover the bottom of the pan. Fry the bread quickly on both sides until crisp.

Cooking time: 5 to 10 minutes
Serves 4

*To make this a healthier recipe, use margarine or vegetable oil instead of bacon fat to fry the bread, and use skim milk.

Mushrooms on Toast

½ lb. fresh mushrooms

2 tbsp. butter*

salt and pepper

1 tbsp. cornstarch

1 c. milk

4 slices buttered toast

1. Wash mushrooms and drain on paper towel. Cut into quarters.

2. Melt butter in a frying pan. Add mushrooms and salt and pepper to taste. Sauté over medium-low heat until soft.

3. While mushrooms are cooking, mix cornstarch with a little of the milk in a small bowl to make a smooth, thin paste. Then add the rest of the milk and stir until mixture is free of lumps.

4. Slowly add milk mixture to mushrooms in the pan, stirring constantly. Cook over low heat for 1 minute.

5. Pour mixture over toast and serve immediately.

Preparation time: 10 minutes
Cooking time: 10 minutes
Serves 4

To reduce the fat, use margarine instead of butter, and use skim milk.

Derbyshire Oatcakes

This recipe comes from the county of Derby (pronounced "Darby") in the Midlands, a region in the middle of England. Oatcakes are popular throughout the Midlands and the north, where oats are grown. Oatcakes are a thick, biscuitlike pancake.

1 c. oatmeal*

1 c. flour

pinch salt

½ to 1 c. water

1 tbsp. baking powder

1. Mix the oatmeal, flour, and salt with the water to form a thin batter. Add the baking powder just before cooking.

2. Grease a large frying pan and heat on high. Pour cupfuls of the batter into the hot pan and cook like thick pancakes for 4 to 5 minutes on each side until golden brown.

3. Serve hot with bacon and eggs or sprinkled with lemon juice and sugar. You can also serve them later, warmed up or toasted with cheese.

Preparation time: 5 minutes
Cooking time: 10 minutes
Serves 4

*Use slow-cooking, rather than instant, oats.

Sunday Lunch

Lunch in England is served between 12:00 and 2:00 P.M. Some families eat their main meal at midday, while others do so in the evening. A hearty lunch may consist of "meat and two veg" and pudding. The meat is often a stew, and the vegetables usually include a starchy one, such as potatoes, and a green one, such as cabbage. On most days, people prefer to eat a lighter lunch, such as fish, a salad, a baked potato (called a jacket potato), or a sandwich.

The most common lunch served at pubs is the "ploughman's lunch," which started as a meal for farmworkers. This is a platter containing cheese (often Cheddar), crusty white or brown bread, butter, and a pickled onion or two.

Sunday lunch is usually a larger and more formal meal. A popular Sunday lunch is a large joint of beef, mutton, or lamb roasted in the oven, accompanied by roast potatoes and other vegetables, with a pudding for dessert.

While English eating habits have changed over the years, a roast joint of beef, with browned roast potatoes and Yorkshire pudding, is still popular on Sundays. (Recipes on pages 38, 39, and 41.)

Roast Beef

This classic English dish is usually served with browned roast potatoes and Yorkshire pudding (recipes on pages 39 and 41).

3½- to 4-lb. boneless sirloin roast, rolled and tied (boneless roasts already rolled and tied are sold in many stores)*

salt and pepper

3 tbsp. vegetable shortening

1. Preheat the oven to 350°F.

2. Sprinkle salt and pepper over roast. Place roast on a wire rack in an open roasting pan with the fat side on top. (In other words, roast should be resting on its edge, not lying flat.) Dot with shortening. Insert a meat thermometer into the center of the roast so that the top of the thermometer does not touch any fat.

3. Roast the beef on the middle rack of the oven for 2 hours or until the meat thermometer registers that roast is done. When beef is rare, the meat thermometer will show 130° to 140°F; when medium, 150° to 160°F; when well done, 160° to 170°F.

Preparation time: 10 minutes
Cooking time: about 2 hours
Serves 4 to 6

When you shop for a beef roast, choose one marked "lean" or "extra lean" for the lowest fat content. However, a roast that is well marbled, or flecked inside with tiny white bits of fat, and that has a thick layer of fat around the outside will be juicier than a very lean roast.

Browned Roast Potatoes

8 medium-sized potatoes

salt

1. Wash and peel potatoes. Put them in a saucepan and barely cover with lightly salted water. Boil until half-cooked (about 10 minutes).

2. Drain potatoes. Place them in the roasting pan around the beef, after it has already been in the oven for 45 minutes. Potatoes should cook for at least 45 minutes to 1 hour. Baste them occasionally with fat drippings from the meat.*

Preparation time: 20 minutes
Cooking time: 45 minutes to 1 hour
Serves 4 to 6

By basting and turning the potatoes occasionally during cooking, they will brown on all sides.

Yorkshire Pudding

½ c. all-purpose flour

1 tsp. baking powder

¼ tsp. salt

pinch of pepper

1 egg

1 c. milk*

2 tbsp. vegetable shortening or beef drippings

¼ c. cold water

To reduce the fat in this recipe, use skim milk in the batter.

1. In a bowl, sift flour and baking powder. Mix in salt and pepper.

2. Make a hollow in the center of flour mixture and crack egg into it. Stir well. Add milk gradually and beat until smooth. Refrigerate at least half an hour.

3. Half an hour before the meal is to be served, heat the oven to 425°F. Move meat to a low shelf in the oven, where the temperature will stay slightly cooler.

4. Put shortening in an 8 × 12-inch baking pan. Melt shortening on top shelf of the oven. Or have an experienced cook help you draw 2 tbsp. of beef drippings from the roasting pan.

5. Pour cold water onto chilled pudding batter and stir well. Then pour mixture into melted shortening or beef drippings in the baking pan. Return pan to top shelf of oven for 20 minutes.

6. Cut Yorkshire pudding into squares and arrange them around roast meat and potatoes. Serve with horseradish sauce, if desired.

Preparation time: 1 hour
Baking time: 20 minutes
Serves 4 to 6

Summer Pudding

1 10-oz. package frozen unsweetened raspberries, thawed

1 10-oz. package frozen unsweetened sliced strawberries, thawed

1 1-lb. package frozen unsweetened blackberries, thawed

1 c. sugar

1 loaf sliced white bread, several days old

whipped cream or nondairy topping (optional)

1. Stir all fruit and sugar together in a large bowl. (Allow frozen fruit to defrost thoroughly.)*

2. Meanwhile, cut the crusts off as many bread slices as you will need to line a deep 2-quart bowl. Cut round pieces for the bottom of the bowl and several overlapping wedges for the sides. Line the bowl with bread and pour in fruit mixture and juices. Cover the top completely with more bread slices.

3. Over top bread slices, put a plate that is small enough to fit inside the rim of the bowl. Place a heavy weight such as a brick or rock on top to press it down firmly. Refrigerate for at least 24 hours.

4. When ready to serve, remove the weight and plate. To unmold pudding, place a serving plate upside down on top of the bowl. Then, grasping the plate and bowl firmly, turn them over quickly. The pudding should slide easily onto the plate. If it doesn't, slide a knife blade around the inside edge to loosen it. Serve with fresh whipped cream.

*Summer pudding is especially good when made with fresh fruit. Use 1 c. fresh raspberries, 1 c. fresh sliced strawberries, and 2 c. fresh blackberries. Sweetened frozen fruit can also be used, but remember to omit the sugar.

Preparation time: 30 minutes
(plus 24 hours refrigeration)
Serves 8

Afternoon Tea

At around four o'clock in the afternoon, it's time for that delightful English custom, afternoon tea. Teatime can be a simple "cuppa" (cup of tea) or a fancy affair with sandwiches, cakes, cookies (called biscuits in England), and scones with jam and thick cream.

The tea itself is usually made in a teapot with loose tea rather than tea bags. The English often make up their own blends with a variety of black teas from India, Sri Lanka, and China. English people put milk (not cream) in their tea and often sugar as well. The following pages include a description of the time-honored ritual of making tea in the English fashion as well as recipes for a few scrumptious goodies to go with it.

A Victoria sandwich, a luscious teatime treat, consists of two layers of light, fluffy sponge cake. Creamy frosting is sandwiched in between the layers, as well as on top. (Recipe on pages 50–51.)

Tea

1 c. water per person

1 tsp. of loose black tea for each person and 1 for the pot (or 1 tea bag for each person and 1 for the pot)*

1. Fill a kettle with cold water. Bring water to boil.

2. Meanwhile, warm the teapot by filling it with hot tap water.

3. When water in the kettle boils, empty the tap water from the teapot. Put in tea by teaspoonful or bag.

4. Fill the teapot with boiling water from the kettle. Be careful not to splash yourself!

5. Allow tea to steep for about 3 minutes. Stir and serve. If using loose tea, pour through a strainer into cups.

Preparation time: 10 minutes
Makes 1 cup per person

Young tea drinkers may prefer tea weakened with extra milk. Hot cocoa, hot apple cider, or warm milk with honey and vanilla are good teatime beverages as well.

Shortbread

margarine or butter for greasing cookie sheet

½ c. (1 stick) softened unsalted butter

3 tbsp. superfine sugar

1 c. all-purpose flour

1. Grease a cookie sheet with margarine or butter and set aside.

2. Beat ½ c. butter and 3 tbsp. sugar to a light, frothy texture. Stir in flour as lightly as possible until mixture is like fine bread crumbs.

3. Turn mixture onto a floured surface and knead gently until it forms a smooth dough.

4. Form dough into a circle 6 inches in diameter and ½-inch thick and transfer it to the cookie sheet. Prick surface of dough lightly with a fork. Refrigerate dough for 20 minutes.

5. Preheat the oven to 350°F. Bake shortbread for 30 minutes. Then turn the oven down to 300°F and bake for 30 to 40 more minutes, until it is crisp and lightly browned.

6. Remove the cookie sheet from the oven. With a sharp knife, cut shortbread into 8 triangles. Let triangles cool slightly on the cookie sheet, then transfer to a wire rack to cool completely.

7. Serve shortbread immediately or store in an airtight container.

Preparation time: 45 minutes
Baking time: 1 hour
Makes 8 triangles

Scones

There are many variations on scones. You can make them with different types of dried fruit, such as cherries or apricots. Savory scones might include Cheddar cheese or chives. You can use the recipe for the scone topping in the hearty autumn hot pot, pages 66–67, by itself to make savory scones.

2 c. all-purpose flour

1 tbsp. baking powder

½ tsp. salt

½ c. butter (1 stick)*

2 tbsp. sugar

1 egg

⅓ c. milk or buttermilk (enough to make a stiff dough)

⅓ c. currants or raisins (if desired)

1. Preheat the oven to 450°F.

2. In a large bowl, sift together flour, baking powder, and salt. Cut in the butter with your fingers as lightly as possible until the mixture resembles bread crumbs. Stir in sugar. Add the egg and mix with a fork. Gradually stir in the milk or buttermilk to form a stiff dough. Mix in currants or raisins, if desired.

3. On a lightly floured surface (such as a board or tabletop), roll dough out until it is ¾-inch thick. Cut into 2-inch circles with a cookie cutter or the rim of a small drinking glass.

4. Place scones on a greased, floured cookie sheet and bake on the middle rack of the oven for about 10 minutes or until the tops are light golden brown.

5. Remove from oven and place on a wire rack. Serve while still warm with butter, jam, and whipped cream, if you like.

*To make low-fat scones, replace the butter in the recipe with about ⅓ c. buttermilk, using enough to make a stiff dough. Another low-fat alternative is to use ½ c. skim milk plus 2 tbsp. melted margarine in place of the butter and milk or buttermilk.

Preparation time: 20 minutes
Baking time: 10 minutes
Makes 12 scones

Victoria Sandwich

Flavoring ingredients (choose one):

Lemon—6 drops lemon extract and grated peel of 1 lemon

Chocolate—3 tbsp. cocoa mixed with enough water or milk to make a stiff paste

Coffee—1 heaping tbsp. instant coffee mixed with 1 tbsp. boiling water

Cake ingredients:

2 eggs

½ c. (1 stick) margarine or butter

½ c. superfine sugar

1 c. plus 2 tbsp. all-purpose flour sifted together with 2 tsp. baking powder

1. Mix flavoring of your choice in a cup and set aside.

2. In a medium bowl, beat eggs with an electric mixer until frothy. In a large bowl, beat margarine or butter and sugar until light and frothy.

3. Add a little egg to margarine/sugar mixture and beat well. Add a little of the flour and baking powder mixture and beat. Repeat alternate additions of egg and flour, beating constantly until all is well blended.

4. Preheat the oven to 375°F. Meanwhile, add flavoring to batter and beat well. Grease and lightly flour the sides and bottom of two 7-inch cake pans about 1½ inches deep.

5. Spoon equal amounts of cake mixture into each pan and spread evenly with a spatula. Make the center a little lower than the sides because the center always rises more.

6. Bake cakes in the middle to upper part of the oven for 20 minutes, or until their edges come away from the pans. Remove from the oven and allow to cool for 10 minutes in the pans. Then tip cakes onto wire racks to cool completely.

Frosting ingredients:

1½ c. powdered sugar

4 tbsp. (½ stick) margarine

flavoring (choose one from list below)

Flavoring ingredients for frosting (choose one):

Lemon—6 drops lemon extract mixed with a little lemon juice and grated peel of half a lemon

Chocolate—1½ tbsp. cocoa sifted together with the powdered sugar and mixed with a little water

Coffee—1 tsp. instant coffee mixed with a little hot water

1. Beat sugar and margarine together with an electric mixer until completely smooth.

2. Mix flavoring of your choice and add sugar/margerine mixture. (For chocolate frosting, you will already have mixed the sugar into the flavoring. Now beat flavoring and margarine together.)

3. To assemble cake, place one cake bottom-side-up on a serving plate and spread the top with half the frosting.

4. Place other cake right-side-up on top and press gently. Then spread the top with remaining frosting.

Preparation time: cake—25 minutes,
(plus 10 minutes to cool)
frosting—10 minutes
Baking time: 20 minutes
Serves 10

Supper

In England, supper can be any meal eaten from 6:00 P.M. to late at night. Only a very formal meal eaten rather late would be called dinner. If supper is eaten before 6:00 P.M., it might be called high tea. This would include a combination of tea and supper dishes. But most people eat supper between 6:00 and 7:00 P.M.

Supper usually consists of a main dish and a dessert. After dessert, people sometimes have cheese and crackers. Coffee is served after dessert, either at the table with the cheese and crackers or by itself in the living room.

Vegetarian shepherd's pie satisfies the appetites of people who don't eat meat but who enjoy traditional English foods. The tofu and walnuts provide protein. (Recipe on pages 56–57.)

Shepherd's Pie

3 large potatoes, peeled and halved

2 tbsp. margarine or butter

salt and pepper to taste

¼ c. milk

1 tbsp. vegetable oil

1 large onion, chopped

1 lb. lean ground beef

1 large carrot, grated

½ tsp. thyme

1 tbsp. chopped fresh parsley

½ clove garlic, finely chopped, or pinch of garlic powder

salt and pepper to taste

1 tbsp. soy sauce

1. Cook potatoes in 2 quarts boiling salted water until soft (about 15 to 20 minutes).

2. Drain off water and add margarine or butter, salt, and pepper. Mash potatoes, adding enough milk to make a smooth mixture. Set aside.

3. Heat oil in a large skillet and sauté onion until soft. Stir in ground beef and then add carrot, thyme, parsley, garlic, salt, and pepper. (Don't use too much salt because soy sauce is salty.) Cook for another 5 minutes. Add soy sauce and stir well.

4. Preheat the oven to 375°F.

5. Spread meat mixture in a deep pie dish. Spread mashed potatoes evenly over meat mixture and swirl with a fork to create an attractive pattern.

6. Bake the pie on the middle rack of the oven for 30 minutes, or until top is lightly browned. Serve immediately.

Preparation time: 50 minutes
Baking time: 30 minutes
Serves 4

Vegetarian Shepherd's Pie

To toast the walnuts, spread them on a cookie sheet or in a metal pie pan. Bake at 350°F for five minutes, or until golden brown.

Tofu layer:

2 tbsp. vegetable oil

I large onion, chopped

¼ tsp. thyme

½ tsp. ground coriander

pinch of black pepper

½ c. walnuts, toasted and chopped

I cake tofu, frozen, thawed, and shredded*

juice of half a lemon (about I tbsp.)

1–2 tbsp. soy sauce

Mashed potato layer:

4 large potatoes, peeled and cubed

3 tbsp. margarine or butter

½ c. milk

salt to taste

1. Heat the oil in a medium-sized frying pan. Sauté the chopped onion in the oil with the thyme, coriander, and pepper until the onions are clear and soft, about 10 minutes. Stir in the chopped walnuts and shredded tofu. When heated through, stir in lemon juice and soy sauce. Remove from heat.

2. To make the layer of mashed potatoes, place the cubed potatoes in a saucepan and cover with lightly salted water. Bring to a boil, then simmer until potatoes are soft (about 8 minutes). Drain, saving the hot potato water to use in the mushroom gravy.

3. Place the potatoes in a large bowl and mash. Add the margerine or butter, milk, and salt. Stir well.

The texture of tofu becomes meatlike when frozen and thawed. To freeze, place the tofu cake in the freezer, uncovered or lightly covered with plastic wrap. Thaw the tofu in the refrigerator for 24 hours or at room temperature for 7 to 8 hours. Gently squeeze the water out of it, then grate it.

Mushroom gravy:

2 tbsp. vegetable oil

½ lb. mushrooms, sliced

3 tbsp. soy sauce

pinch of pepper

1½ c. hot potato water

2 tbsp. cornstarch dissolved in ½ c. water

4. For the gravy, heat the vegetable oil in a skillet. Stir in the mushrooms, soy sauce, and pepper. Sauté, stirring occasionally, until the mushrooms are tender. Add hot potato water and bring to a boil. Slowly stir in the cornstarch mixture and cook at a low boil, continuing to stir, until the gravy is clear and thick.

5. Preheat the oven to 400°F.

6. Oil a 9-inch-square casserole dish. Spread the tofu mixture across the bottom of the dish, followed by the mushroom gravy and the mashed potatoes. Dot the top with butter or margarine. Bake at 400°F for 15 to 20 minutes until the top becomes golden.

Preparation time: 50 minutes
Baking time: 20 minutes
Serves 4

Poached Fish

2 tbsp. margarine or butter

1½ lb. halibut, haddock, or cod*

salt and pepper

1 c. milk

1. Preheat the oven to 375°F.

2. Smear margarine or butter on the bottom and sides of a deep baking dish and lay fish in the bottom. Sprinkle with salt and pepper and pour milk over all.

3. Cover dish with foil and bake on the middle oven rack for 40 minutes. If you are not making the sauce, fish is now ready to serve.

Sauce ingredients:

2 tsp. cornstarch

2 tbsp. milk

2 tbsp. chopped fresh parsley

1 tsp. lemon juice

1. When fish is cooked, remove the pan from the oven. With a spoon or baster, draw off all the liquid into a small saucepan. (Turn down the oven to 200°F and return fish to oven to keep warm.)

2. Bring liquid in the saucepan to a boil over moderate heat.

3. In a cup, mix cornstarch and milk together to make a smooth, thin paste. Gradually pour cornstarch paste into boiling liquid, stirring constantly to prevent lumps. Add parsley and lemon juice. Pour sauce over fish and serve immediately.

Fish steaks work better than fillets, as they hold their shape during the cooking process.

Preparation time: 5 minutes
Cooking time: 45–50 minutes
Serves 4

Holiday and Festival Food

Holidays and festivals in England are a time for families and friends to get together and enjoy a break from work or school. In many towns and villages, people take part in customs that have been around for centuries, whether it's the colorful flash and lively beat of morris dancing or the bonfire on Guy Fawkes Night.

Food often takes center stage during holiday celebrations. Perhaps the most famous holiday fare is Christmas pudding, a steamed dessert filled with dried fruits, such as plums and currants, and topped with a sweet sauce. At Easter, English cooks bake many types of sweets, such as hot cross buns or Easter biscuits. In Cornwall, an Easter specialty is bright yellow saffron buns, made with a spice that comes from the crocus flower.

The following recipes have special connections to holidays or seasons. After you taste them, you'll agree that they're too good to save for just once a year.

Wassail punch is a favorite beverage during the Christmas holidays. (Recipe on page 69.)

61

Carlings

Carlings are dried peas, a traditional meal for Lent in Yorkshire. It's said that whoever gets the last pea in the pot will be the first to get married.

8 oz. dried green peas

3 c. cold water

2 to 3 tbsp. fresh bread crumbs

1 medium onion, finely chopped

¼ tsp. thyme

¼ tsp. rosemary

salt and black pepper to taste

1 tbsp. melted butter

flour

1 tbsp. butter for frying

1. Soak peas overnight in cold water.

2. The next morning, drain peas and rinse well. Place peas in a large saucepan and cover with 3 c. cold water.

3. Bring water to boil and cook peas for 1½ to 2 hours, stirring regularly and adding extra water if necessary, until the peas are tender.

4. Drain and allow peas to cool. Then, in a large bowl, mix the peas with the bread crumbs, onion, herbs, salt and pepper, and melted butter to form a stiff mixture.

5. Shape mixture into cakes and dust lightly with flour. Melt 1 tbsp. of butter in a frying pan and fry the carlings until golden brown, turning once. Serve immediately.

Preparation time: 10 minutes
(plus soaking overnight)
Cooking time: 2½ to 3 hours
Serves 4

Easter Biscuits

These spicy fruited biscuits, which Americans call cookies, were originally baked for Easter in the West Country.

½ c. (1 stick) butter

½ c. superfine sugar

1 egg, separated

1 c. flour

¼ tsp. ground allspice

¼ tsp. ground cloves

¼ c. currants

2 tsp. grated orange peel*

1 tsp. grated lemon peel*

2 tbsp. milk

sugar for sprinkling

1. Preheat the oven to 400°F.

2. Cream the butter and sugar together until pale and fluffy. Beat in egg yolk (save the egg white for step 4). Sift in the flour and spices and mix well. Add the currants and orange and lemon peel and enough milk to form a soft dough.

3. Turn dough onto a floured surface (such as a board or tabletop) and knead gently. Roll out to about ½-inch thickness. Cut into 2-inch circles (use a cookie cutter or the rim of a small drinking glass). Prick the tops with a fork.

4. Put biscuits onto two greased baking sheets. Bake for 10 minutes. Remove from oven. Brush with lightly beaten egg white, sprinkle with sugar, and return to oven. Bake for about 5 minutes longer, until the tops are golden brown. Transfer to wire racks to cool. Store in an airtight container.

Use a grater, a potato peeler, or a zester to gently remove peel in small pieces from the lemon and orange. Try to avoid getting the white pith, which has a bitter taste. You can chop or mince the peel with a knife for even smaller pieces.

Preparation time: 20 minutes
Baking time: 15 minutes
Makes 30 biscuits

Hearty Autumn Hot Pot

Use this dish to celebrate the fall harvest season.

Stew ingredients:

4 tbsp. margarine or butter

2 medium onions, sliced

4 medium carrots, sliced

2 parsnips, cut into chunks

1 small cauliflower, cut into florets

4 zucchini, sliced

6 tomatoes, skinned and coarsely
　　chopped*

¼ c. flour

1¼ c. milk

1¼ c. vegetable stock

½ tsp. thyme

½ tsp. oregano

1 tsp. salt

½ tsp. black pepper

1. Preheat the oven to 400°F.

2. Melt 4 tbsp. margarine or butter in a large saucepan. Add the onions, carrots, and parsnips and sauté lightly for 5 minutes. Transfer to a large casserole dish. Add the remaining vegetables.

3. Blend the flour with the milk and add to the vegetables with the vegetable stock, herbs, and salt and pepper. Mix well. Bake on the center rack of the oven for 40 minutes.

4. Meanwhile, make the scones. Place the whole wheat flour, baking powder, and salt in a medium bowl. Cut in 2 tbsp. butter or margarine to flour until the mixture resembles fine bread crumbs. Stir in half the cheese, the dry mustard, and enough milk to make a soft dough.

5. Turn dough onto a lightly floured surface and roll to ¾-inch thickness. Cut into 2-inch circles (use a cookie cutter or the rim of a small drinking glass).

*To peel a tomato, place it in a small saucepan of boiling water for about 1 minute. Remove with a slotted spoon and cool until the tomato is warm but no longer hot. Use a small paring knife to peel off the skin. It will come off easily.

Scone ingredients:

⅔ c. whole wheat flour

I tsp. baking powder

½ tsp. salt

2 tbsp. butter or margarine

½ c. grated Cheddar cheese

I tsp. dry mustard

about ½ c. milk*

6. Remove the casserole from oven and place scones on top of the vegetables. Brush tops of scones with milk and sprinkle with the remaining cheese.

7. Return to oven for 20 minutes until scones are golden brown and vegetables are cooked.

Preparation time: 30 minutes
Baking time: 1 hour
Serves 6

You can reduce the fat in this recipe by using skim milk, reduced-fat cheese, and margarine instead of butter.

Gingerbread

Gingerbread is traditionally eaten around the bonfire on Guy Fawkes Night, but it's delicious throughout the winter months.

shortening or margarine

1⅔ c. flour

1 tbsp. ground ginger

1 tbsp. ground allspice

½ tsp. salt

2 tsp. baking powder

1 tsp. baking soda

½ c. (1 stick) unsalted butter

½ c. packed dark brown sugar

3 eggs

⅔ c. molasses

1. Preheat the oven to 325°F. Grease the bottom and sides of an 8-inch-square cake pan. Follow this with a light dusting of flour, shaking out any excess. Set aside.

2. Sift the flour, ginger, allspice, salt, baking powder, and baking soda into a bowl.

3. In another bowl, cream the butter and brown sugar until very soft. Beat in the eggs one by one, then mix in the molasses. Gently fold in the dry ingredients.

4. Pour the mixture into the prepared pan. Bake for 50 to 60 minutes, or until the top springs back when pressed lightly with your fingertips.

5. Cool in the pan, then remove and store in an airtight container.

Preparation time: 20 minutes
Baking time: 50 to 60 minutes
Makes 8–12 pieces

Wassail Punch

This nonalcoholic version of wassail punch is very tasty. It's a perfect way to keep out the cold on a frosty winter night.

5 qts. apple cider

7 tbsp. brown sugar

3 sliced oranges

4 whole cloves

¼ tsp. nutmeg

¼ tsp. cinnamon

2 bananas, thinly sliced

1. In a large kettle, heat the cider slowly with the sugar, sliced oranges, and spices until it is almost boiling.

2. Pour into a punch bowl, add the bananas, and serve at once.*

Preparation time: 25 minutes
Serves 10 to 12

Tall glass mugs or glass cups show off the colorful brew.

Index

About the Author

Barbara W. Hill was born in London and grew up in Rugby, England. She went to schools in Rugby and Oxford before attending art college. She and her husband spent two years in Sweden and then moved to Northfield, Minnesota. Hill is a professional artist who specializes in printmaking and painting.

Hill first learned to cook from her mother. She often delights her friends with English meals and takes great pleasure in both the preparation and presentation of the meals.